'One year of this is enough!'

Cornerstones of Freedom

The Story of
WATERGATE

By Jim Hargrove

CHILDRENS PRESS ®
CHICAGO

Republican National Convention in Miami, Florida, August 23, 1972

Page 2: The Caucus Room of the Senate, the site of
the Watergate hearings

Library of Congress Cataloging-in-Publication Data

Hargrove, Jim.
    The story of Watergate.

    (Cornerstones of freedom)
    Includes index.
    Summary: Synthesizes the biggest political scandal
in United States history, a series of activities
attempting to help Richard M. Nixon win reelection in
1972.
    1.   Watergate Affair, 1972-1974—Juvenile literature.
[1.   Watergate Affair, 1972-1974]   I.   Title.
II.   Series.
E860.H37   1988   364.1'32'0973   88-11881
ISBN 0-516-04741-8

Children's Press®, Chicago
Copyright © 1988 by Regensteiner Publishing Enterprises, Inc.
All rights reserved. Printed in the United States of America.
Weekly Reader is a trademark of Field Publications.

On the evening of August 23, 1972, President Richard M. Nixon felt on top of the world. Republicans at the National Convention in Miami Beach, Florida, had just voted 1,347 to 1 to nominate him to run for a second term in the White House.

There was another reason for Nixon's satisfaction. A little more than a month earlier, members of the Democratic Party had met, also in Miami Beach, to choose their own presidential candidate. They had selected George McGovern, a United States senator. McGovern was the very man Nixon and his aides most wanted to run against. The Republicans were certain that they could beat the senator, and they were absolutely right.

George McGovern greets supporters at a rally in San Francisco.

President Nixon and Vice President Agnew wave to the cheering crowd after their reelection.

On November 7, 1972, Nixon won the presidential election by, at the time, the biggest Republican landslide in history. Forty-nine states voted for Nixon. Only Massachusetts and the District of Columbia went to Senator McGovern. But the victorious Nixon had little time to enjoy his victory. His world, and the world of most of his top advisers, was beginning to turn upside down.

Over a period of about two years, newspaper reporters, judges, lawyers, congressmen, and government investigators slowly pieced together the shocking story of Nixon's reelection. They discovered that people working for the President had written lies about leading Democrats in order to keep them from running against him. They found that millions of dollars had been illegally obtained and spent for Nixon's reelection. They also learned that many of the administration's top officials, possibly including the President himself, had broken the law trying to hide their crimes from public view.

More than thirty people working for the Nixon administration broke the law. Most served time in jail. President Nixon was not convicted of anything. But the scandal eventually forced him to become the first American president to resign from office. Had he not voluntarily stepped down, he almost certainly would have been impeached. The scandal that toppled an administration and threatened America's government began with little hint of the serious consequences that would follow.

Overlooking the Potomac River and the Kennedy Center for the Performing Arts in Washington, D.C., is a group of six large buildings. Known as Watergate, the modern complex is made up of a hotel and several office and apartment buildings. At the time, the Democratic National Committee had rented the entire sixth floor of the Watergate office building as a national headquarters.

Watergate complex

At about 2 A.M. on Saturday, June 17, 1972, five suspected burglars wearing surgical gloves and carrying walkie-talkies were arrested in the Democratic headquarters by Washington police. Those arrested were James W. McCord, who was a resident of the Washington area, and four Cuban Americans. When the Washington police learned that the suspects were staying at the Watergate Hotel, they obtained search warrants and began looking through the rooms. The police quickly knew that they had arrested some unusual burglars. The police found large numbers of electronic listening and telephone-tapping devices, small tear-gas guns,

Tools found on the Watergate burglars included screwdrivers, lock picks, and false identification.

rolls of unexposed film, burglary tools, cameras, and walkie-talkies. Apparently the burglars were engaged in a plan to illegally spy on Democratic headquarters.

The police turned up $4,500 in new, one-hundred-dollar bills. Apparently someone had paid the burglars to do the deed.

The police discovered a bank check signed by an E. Howard Hunt and a small notebook in which "H. H.—W. House" was written. Had someone with the initials *H. H.* at the White House been involved?

Investigation showed that this was the second time the burglars had broken into headquarters. A month earlier they had entered the Watergate offices and installed secret electronic listening devices, or "bugs." Someone was using these bugs to hear the Democrats discuss plans to win forthcoming elections. What was heard would be valuable to an opponent of the Democrats.

When they were caught, the burglars had been breaking in the second time to adjust the "bugs."

Few people thought about the news report on the break-in buried in the back pages of a daily newspaper on Saturday. But the same weekend that the burglary occurred, reporters discovered that one of the arrested burglars, James W. McCord, worked as the security chief for the Committee to Reelect the President, soon called CREEP. The Committee to Reelect the President had been formed in 1971 by Nixon and some of his top aides. A similar organization, the Finance Committee to Reelect the President was also formed to raise campaign funds. Could members of Nixon's committees be responsible for the Watergate break-in?

CREEP was directed by John N. Mitchell, a former U.S. Attorney General in Nixon's cabinet who had resigned his post in order to manage the president's reelection. By Sunday, June 18, just one day after the Watergate break-in, Mitchell issued a statement. "McCord and the other four men arrested in Democratic headquarters Saturday were not operating either in our behalf or with our consent in the alleged bugging," Mitchell said. "There is no place in our campaign or in the electoral process for this type of activity, and we will not permit or condone it."

Mitchell was lying. He was already trying hard to hide CREEP's involvement in the burglary. One White House official charged that he had ordered the burglary in the first place, although Mitchell denied it.

Among the people who soon found Mitchell's statements hard to believe were two young reporters for the *Washington Post* newspaper, Bob Wood-

Attorney General John N. Mitchell (below right) before the Senate subcommittee. Carl Bernstein (left) and Bob Woodward (below right) won the Pulitzer Prize for breaking the story on the Watergate scandal.

ward and Carl Bernstein. Assigned to the story of the unusual break-in by their editor, Woodward and Bernstein began digging. They wanted to learn more about the connection between the burglary and officials in CREEP and, possibly, even people in the White House.

Led by the determined investigations of Woodward and Bernstein, the nation's newspapers soon revealed additional surprising information about the burglary. The break-in had been directed not by any of the men arrested, but by two others. These two had been inside the Watergate building at the time of the break-in but had not been caught by police. One man was G. Gordon Liddy, a former Federal Bureau of Investigation (FBI) agent and the legal advisor to the Finance Committee to Reelect the President. The other was E. Howard Hunt, a former Central Intelligence Agency (CIA) agent and a con-

G. Gordon Liddy (left) and E. Howard Hunt (right) were accused of planning the Watergate break-in.

President Nixon held a press conference at the Western White House in San Clemente, California, on August 29, 1972

sultant paid directly by the White House. The letters *H. H.* written in the notebook found at Watergate probably referred to Howard Hunt, and *W. House* certainly meant White House. The reporters discovered that the crisp one-hundred-dollar bills the burglars possessed had come from Nixon campaign contributions.

At a news conference held on August 29, 1972, less than a week after his renomination, President Nixon declared that no one in the administration had anything to do with Watergate. The President pointed out that a lawyer on his staff, John Dean, had conducted a complete Watergate investigation.

"I can state categorically," the President said, "that his investigation indicates that no one in the

White House staff, no one in this Administration, presently employed, was involved in this very bizarre incident." Strangely enough, John Dean later testified that this was the first he had heard about his own report.

The President was actually voicing some wishful thinking at his press conference. He had ample reason to wish that his administration had not been involved in the burglary and that investigations into it would stop. After all, he had just been renominated for the presidency by the Republican party. With the elections little more than two months away, he wanted Watergate to be put to rest. By mid-September that almost happened.

On September 15 a Washington grand jury charged seven men with crimes associated with the Watergate burglary. The men charged were G. Gordon Liddy and E. Howard Hunt (the two men who had planned the operation) and the five men cap-

E. Howard Hunt

G. Gordon Liddy

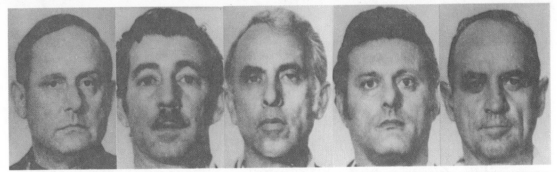

From left to right: Bernard Barker, Virgilio Gonzalez, Eugenio Martinez, Frank Sturgis, James McCord Jr.

tured by Washington police on the night of the break-in. To the great relief of the Nixon administration, nobody who actually worked inside the White House was accused of a crime.

Many people, including Democratic politicians and newspaper reporters, wondered whether the charges had reached an end. Probably more people had been involved than had been caught. But the administration would fight new accusations. Attorney General Richard Kleindienst insisted that the FBI had made "one of the most intensive, objective,

Attorney General Richard Kleindienst

and thorough" investigations in years when it had looked into the Watergate affair.

The FBI investigation had been carried out by 333 agents in fifty-one offices throughout the country. The agents had developed 1,897 leads, conducted 1,551 interviews, and spent 14,098 hours on the case. Considering time spent on the investigation, it was remarkable that the FBI did not arrive at the truth about Watergate. Only much later was it learned that President Nixon and his aides had used the CIA to keep the FBI investigators from finding out a lot of valuable information.

The glowing praise for the FBI investigation kept many Americans from suspecting that people very close to the President were guilty in Watergate. Americans in droves voted for President Nixon in the elections of November 1972. But from the beginning of Nixon's second term in office, the scandal grew and grew.

The seven men charged by the Washington grand jury with Watergate-related crimes went on trial on January 8, 1973. Presiding at the Washington district court trial was Judge John Sirica, a Republican, known for fairness. Early in the sixteen-day trial, five of the defendants pleaded guilty to burglary, conspiracy, and illegal wiretapping. The remaining two were convicted of the same crimes by the jury.

Convicted Watergate conspirator James McCord (left) shows the Watergate Committee how to bug a telephone. Judge John J. Sirica (right) presided over the Watergate trial.

Not one of the defendants took the witness stand to speak for himself. One of the defendants, CREEP security chief James W. McCord, later said that he had been pressured to plead guilty and remain silent about others involved. A member of CREEP had told McCord "The President's ability to govern is at stake . . . and the government may fall. Everybody else is on track but you, you are not following the game plan." McCord also said he was assured that the President would grant a pardon if he was sentenced to a jail term.

Judge Sirica was dissatisfied. He felt that attorneys were not pressing hard enough for answers to simple questions such as: Who hired the burglars? What were they looking for? The trial ended on January 30, 1973, but Judge Sirica delayed sentencing until March 23.

17

In the meantime, on February 7, 1973, the U.S. Senate had voted to create a Senate Select Committee to investigate the Watergate affair. It also was to look for illegality in the presidential election of 1972. Chosen to head the committee was Democratic Senator Sam Ervin from North Carolina. For some months members of the Ervin committee worked behind the scenes with staff lawyers, researchers, witnesses, and other government agents before beginning public hearings in May.

While the senators led by Ervin were doing this background work, the March 23 sentencing date for the convicted Watergate burglars arrived. Judge Sirica read a letter from defendant and CREEP worker James McCord. McCord stated that White House officials had been conducting a cover-up to hide their own involvement in the Watergate scandal. He also charged that the defendants had been pressured by the White House into pleading guilty and not revealing all they knew. He added that witnesses had lied under oath.

Judge Sirica sentenced G. Gordon Liddy, legal adviser to the Finance Committee to Reelect the President and one of the two planners of the break-in, to prison for a period not less than 6 years 8 months nor more than 20 years. The judge gave the other 6 defendants unusually harsh sentences of 35 to 40 years in jail. However, the judge said that the sentences might be reduced if the defendants cooperated with a continuing Watergate investigation.

McCord's testimony caused the White House cover-up of the break-in to begin unraveling. An assistant to former CREEP director John Mitchell admitted that he had lied under oath. He now said that the break-in had been approved by CREEP officials. Mitchell and John Dean, the president's lawyer, had urged him to lie under oath.

A number of witnesses, including John Dean, accused the President's closest advisors of having participated in Watergate. A witness said that John Mitchell had approved the break-in in advance. Witnesses also said that typed versions of conversations illegally overheard at Democratic headquarters had been given to H. R. Haldeman, the President's chief of staff. One of Nixon's top advisors, John Ehrlich-

resident Richard M. Nixon

H. R. Haldeman

John D. Ehrlichman

man, was accused of ordering the destruction of documents relating to the scandal.

In a televised address on April 30, 1973, President Nixon admitted that "there had been an effort to conceal the facts." Insisting he had no personal involvement in the cover-up or the break-in, Nixon blamed everything on his staff. He announced the resignations of Ehrlichman and Haldeman, and said that he had fired legal adviser Dean. Preferring not to prosecute people he had worked with, Attorney General Kleindienst resigned at the same time.

If the Watergate scandal had been a fairy tale instead of a real-life tragedy, President Nixon's nose might have grown ten feet long during that April 30th speech. He had known about the cover-up nearly from the beginning. Later, it was learned that more than a month before that same speech, Nixon had told former CREEP director John Mitchell, "I want you all to stonewall it [the investigation], let them plead the Fifth Amendment, cover-up or anything else, if it'll save it—save the plan . . . . Up to this point, the whole theory has been containment, as you know, John."

When Attorney General Kleindienst resigned, Nixon appointed a replacement, Elliott Richardson. Richardson and Nixon agreed to create a special prosecutor's office headed by Harvard Law School

The Senate Select Committee held televised hearings. Senator Sam Ervin is fifth from the right.

professor Archibald Cox to investigate the scandal more thoroughly. In the meantime, Senator Sam Ervin's Senate Select Committee began its televised hearings.

Senator Ervin had made arrangements to hold the Watergate hearings in the Senate's historic Caucus Room. That large room had been the scene of hearings on earlier government scandals, including Teapot Dome and the Army-McCarthy controversy.

On Thursday morning, May 17, 1973, the hearings began in a room cluttered with television and motion picture cameras, microphones, bright lights, still photographers, reporters, and other people.

For much of the summer, daytime television viewers throughout America found their steady diet of soap operas and quiz shows suddenly, and dramatically, altered. All the major television networks dropped their normal programs and televised the Senate hearings. Many people found the hearings fascinating. It was a chance to see government officials in action.

One by one, all of the major actors in the Watergate drama were called upon to testify before the committee. Bit by bit, more pieces of the puzzle were discovered and placed before the American people. A disturbing picture was created. It helped to explain how Nixon had won by a landslide in 1972.

One of the most important discoveries was that Republican campaign workers tried to ruin the chances of Democratic presidential candidates. In June of 1971, two White House staff members hired a young lawyer named Donald Segretti. Segretti's job was to play dirty tricks on Democratic presidential hopefuls.

At the time, Senator Edmund Muskie of Maine was considered by many to be the leading candidate to win the Democratic presidential nomination. Some public opinion polls indicated that he could beat President Nixon. It was young Segretti's task to make certain that such a thing did not happen.

Senator Jackson (left) displays a copy of a letter that Donald Segretti (right) had distributed in Florida.

Segretti knew that saying bad things about one Democratic candidate would damage the chances of all Democratic candidates.

In March of 1972 prior to the Florida primary, Segretti wrote a letter. He made it seem as if the letter had been written by a member of Muskie's staff. The letter falsely claimed that one of Muskie's Democratic challengers had been guilty of homosexual acts and of fathering an illegitimate child. The letter claimed that another Democratic opponent, in the company of a prostitute, had been arrested for drunk driving.

All the accusations were false, as was the indication that they came from Senator Muskie. But the

23

distasteful letter had an impact on Florida's Democratic voters. It ruined the election for Muskie.

This is just one of dozens of underhanded activities Segretti directed to destroy the campaigns of many Democrats who hoped to be elected president. He testified that he had twenty-eight agents working for him in twelve different states. He also said that he was paid by a man who worked directly for President Nixon.

Other Republicans had their own dirty tricks. E. Howard Hunt, who had helped to mastermind the Watergate break-in, tried to attack Democrats by discrediting slain president John Kennedy. Hunt faked a State Department telegram, trying to make it appear that Kennedy had ordered the 1963 assassination of the president of South Vietnam.

A number of legal experts have argued about whether these activities were crimes or simply nasty tricks. For his activities, dirty trickster Segretti served a brief prison term.

There is little doubt that the reelection committees handled campaign contributions in illegal ways. CREEP received large contributions, often in cash, from companies and business executives by promising presidential favors. The money, often hidden in safes and in secret bank accounts, was used to finance the Watergate break-in, to keep people from telling the truth, and to pay for political dirty tricks.

It was learned that White House officials had circulated an enemies list, names of people supposedly against President Nixon. It was hard to take the list as a serious threat to government. It included celebrities such as Carol Channing, an actress, and Joe Namath, the quarterback of the New York Jets. Namath said that he was proud to have made the list. Channing, recalling she had once given the Nixons a gift of jewelry, joked that she must have been put on the list after President Nixon had the jewelry appraised. Not so funny, however, was the apparent attempt of White House officials to use government agencies such as the Internal Revenue Service to harass political enemies.

Yet another scandal was discovered during the Watergate investigation. In 1971 President Nixon had organized a special task force known as the plumbers unit. The purpose of the group was to stop secret information from being discovered by reporters. In one case, the plumbers unit illegally broke into the office of a psychiatrist. They found out information about a patient who had given secret Pentagon papers to the *New York Times* newspaper.

Most of these scandals were uncovered as part of the wide-ranging investigation into the Watergate burglary. But as witnesses continued to testify

John Dean (left) testified in the Senate Caucus room (right).

before Senator Ervin's select committee, one part of the puzzle failed to fall into place. What was Nixon's role in Watergate?

In lengthy testimony, John Dean, the president's lawyer, said that Nixon had participated in the cover-up of the Watergate break-in. Most of the president's other top aides denied or refused to support Dean's accusations. Several said that they could not respond to questions put to them because the answers would "endanger national security." It was difficult to know whom to believe.

On July 16, 1973, Alexander Butterfield, a former White House assistant, testified before the Ervin committee and revealed an astounding fact. Since

1970 audio tape recordings had been made in secret. The recordings contained most of the President's discussions conducted in the White House face to face or over the telephone. The tapes would tell who was telling the truth.

On July 23, 1973, both the Ervin committee and special prosecutor Cox demanded the tapes. Nixon refused to supply them, offering written summaries instead. Cox rejected the offer and continued pushing for the tapes. In a desperate move Nixon fired Cox and replaced him with Leon Jaworski, a Texas lawyer. With the firing of Cox it became clear to many people that the President was trying to obstruct justice. Many politicians of both major parties began to suggest that the President should be

Senator Sam Ervin (below) signs subpoenas requesting presidential papers and tapes. Copy of letter (right) Nixon sent to the Watergate Committee refusing to send the tapes.

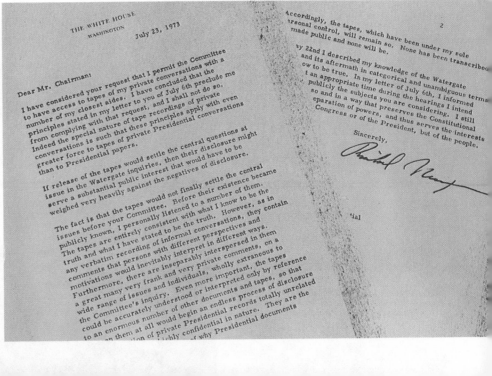

impeached. Under pressure from all sides, Nixon finally released some of the tapes. But one of them contained an eighteen-minute gap that experts claimed was not made accidentally—the tape had been erased. The new special prosecutor, Leon Jaworski, demanded sixty-four more tapes, as did the House Judiciary Committee, whose members were already considering impeaching Nixon.

Instead of complying with the demand, on April 30, 1974, the White House released 1,308 typed pages of transcript, the words spoken on the tapes put down in writing. Many people were amazed by the tone of the conversations in the White House. Instead of considering what was best for the country, Nixon and his advisers talked about what would make the President look good. Many people

Edited versions of President Nixon's taped conversations (right) were turned over to the House Judiciary Committee.

'How about this? While Rose Mary Woods answered the phone, a mouse accidentally ran back and forth across the tape recorder keyboard five to nine times.'

Tourist in front of the Supreme Court reads about the court's ruling ordering President Nixon to release the tapes.

expressed anger that Nixon and his aides frequently used swear words. The phrase "expletive deleted" was sprinkled throughout the transcripts to show that undesirable words had been left out.

The typed transcripts were unacceptable to special prosecutor Jaworski. When the White House refused to surrender the actual tapes, Jaworski asked the U.S. Supreme Court to act. On July 24, 1974, the Court ordered Nixon to release the tapes. The President agreed to surrender them within the next ten days. The order was the final blow to Nixon's presidency. One of the tapes, made on July 23, 1972, clearly proved that he had conspired with his aides to undercut the FBI investigation.

But before the tapes were released, the House

Garner S. Cline (left), associate general counsel, holds the tally sheet of the committee's vote of 27 to 11 to recommend impeachment of the President. President Nixon (right) resigned during a televised speech.

Judiciary Committee voted to impeach Nixon. Three articles of impeachment were approved. The first charged President Nixon with obstructing justice during the Watergate investigation. The second stated that Nixon had abused the powers of the presidency. The final article charged that he had unconstitutionally defied congressional demands for evidence.

For a few days Nixon hoped that he could survive impeachment. But on August 5, 1974, his conversations aimed at halting the FBI's 1972 Watergate investigation were made public. His remaining support in Congress virtually vanished.

Rather than face an impeachment trial, President Nixon decided to resign. Three days later on the evening of August 8, 1974, he gave a short speech on television announcing that he would be leaving the presidency at noon the following day. By the evening of August 9, he was a private citizen living in California. About a month later, President Gerald R. Ford pardoned Nixon for any crimes he might have committed while in office. Had he not been pardoned, Nixon might have faced years of lawsuits.

The Watergate scandal placed the country in turmoil. Extremely important political leaders were convicted of crimes. Many Americans lost confidence in their political leaders. People in other countries lost faith in the United States.

Nevertheless, the scandal proved that the American system of government works. The nation was able to stop the abuse of presidential power. The free press, the concerned public, Congress, and the Supreme Court acted to help the country overcome a massive crisis.

Watergate showed President Nixon at his worst. There are many, many examples of how he served his country well. Unfortunately, they are not a part of the story of Watergate.

Surrounded by his family, President Nixon says farewell.

PHOTO CREDITS

About the Author

   Jim Hargrove has worked as a writer and editor for more than ten years. After serving as an editorial director for three Chicago area publishers, he began a career as an independent writer, preparing a series of books for children. He has contributed to works by nearly twenty different publishers. His Childrens Press titles include biographies of Mark Twain, Daniel Boone, Thomas Jefferson, Lyndon B. Johnson, and Richard Nixon. With his wife and daughter, he lives in a small Illinois town near the Wisconsin border.